SCHIRMER'S LIBRARY
OF MUSICAL CLASSICS

Vol. 1997

ROBERT SCHUMANN

Sonatas

For Piano

Edited by
CLARA SCHUMANN

ISBN 978-0-7935-3068-7

G. SCHIRMER, Inc.

DISTRIBUTED BY

HAL•LEONARD®
CORPORATION
7777 W. BLUEMOUND RD. P.O. BOX 13819 MILWAUKEE, WI 53213

CONTENTS

SONATA No. 1

dedicated to Clara
by
Florestan and Eusebius

Robert Schumann, Op.11
(completed 1835)

Introduzione
Un poco Adagio

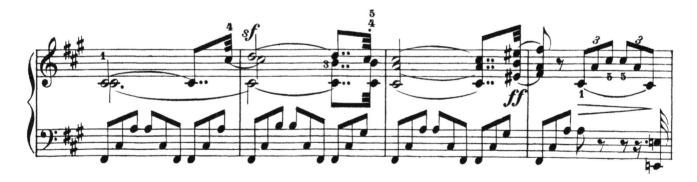

2

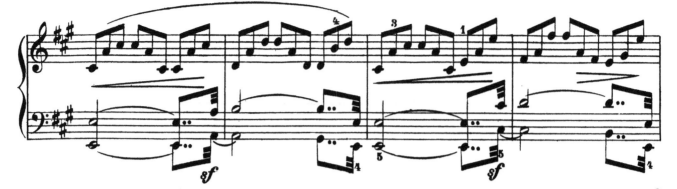

4

Allegro vivace

poco a

poco crescendo

ff

p

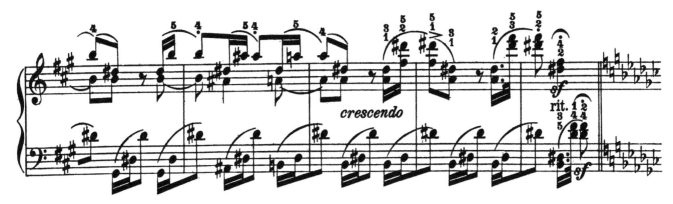

crescendo

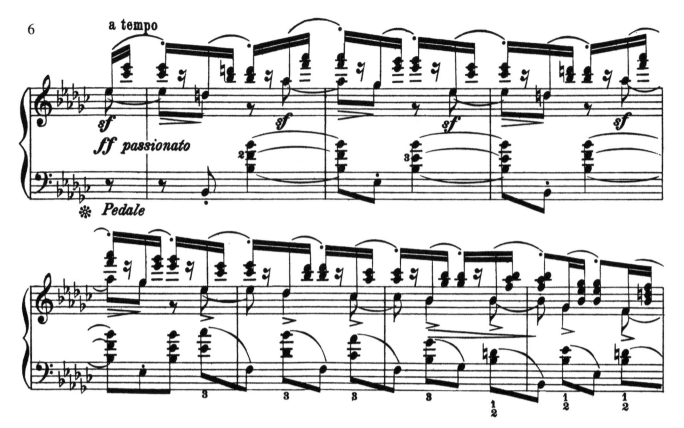

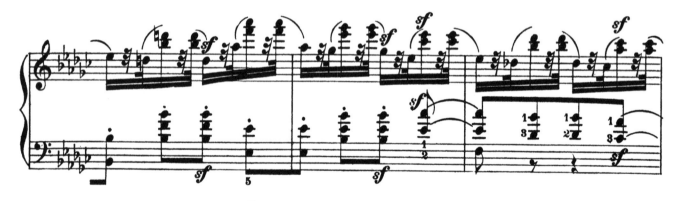

Più lento

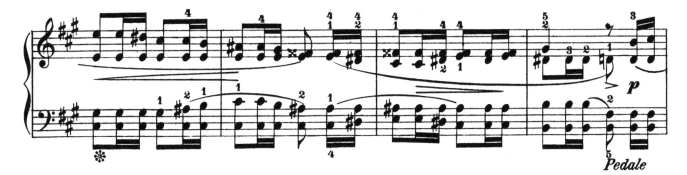

un poco ritenuto   a tempo

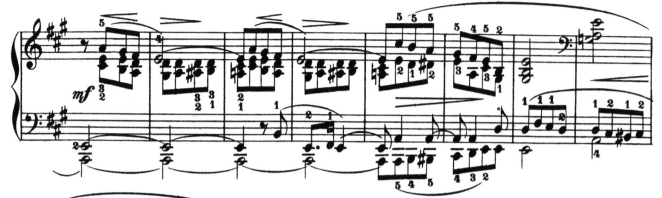

poco piu lento

sempre *p*

Pedale

p

vivacissimo

p

mf

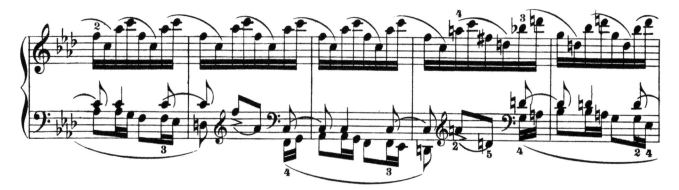

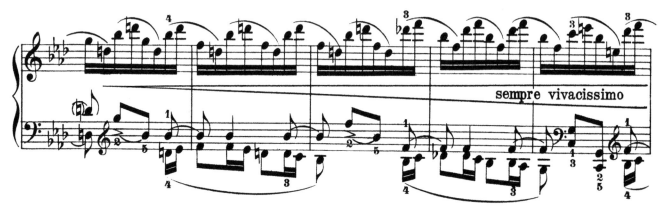

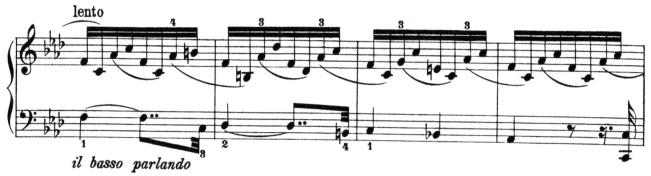

13

ARIA

senza passione, ma espressivo

Pedale

(Ped. giusto)

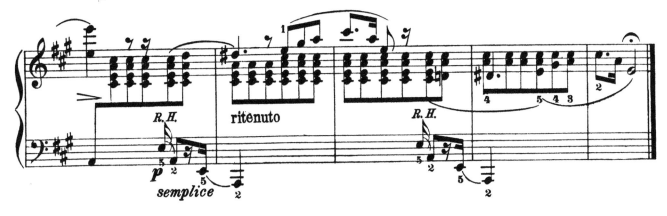

SCHERZO e INTERMEZZO
Allegrissimo

Pedale

marcatissimo

a tempo

legato

i *Bassi vivi*

un poco accelerando

scherzando

INTERMEZZO

Lento *Alla burla, ma pomposo*

FINALE
Allegro un poco maestoso

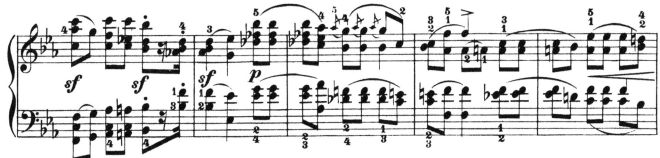

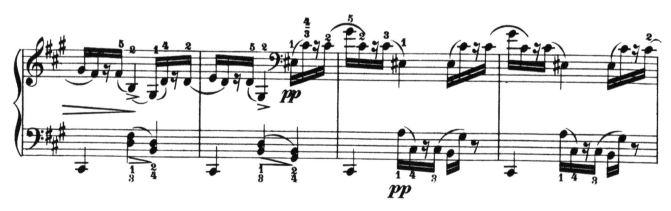

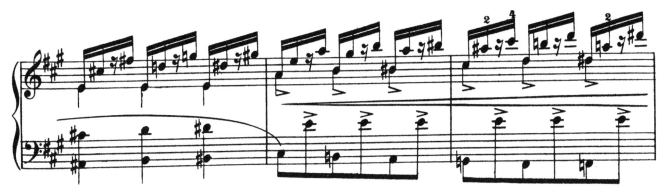

brillante e veloce

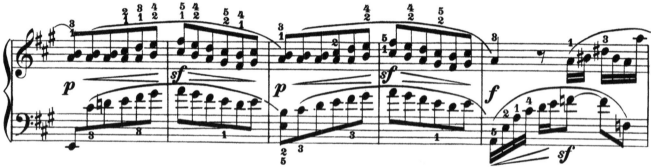

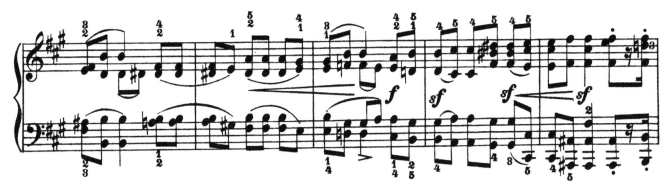

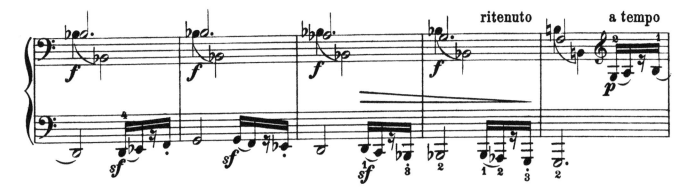

Un poco più lento

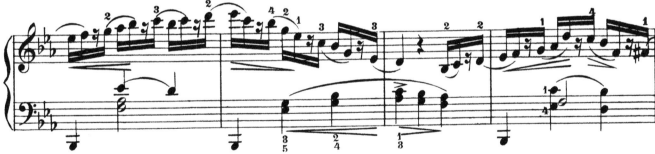

a tempo

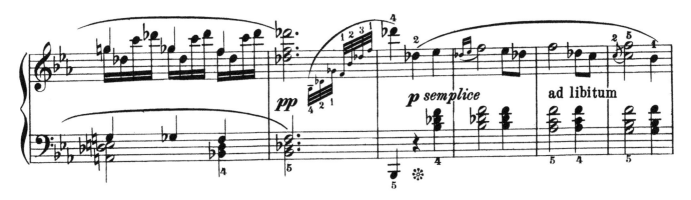

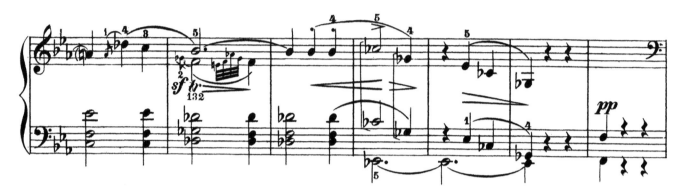

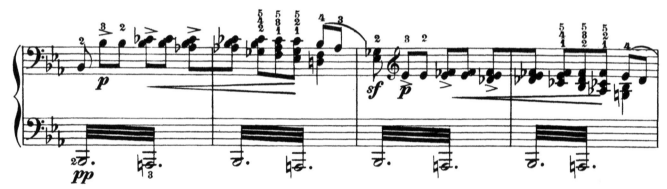

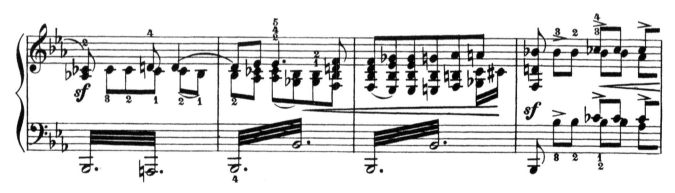

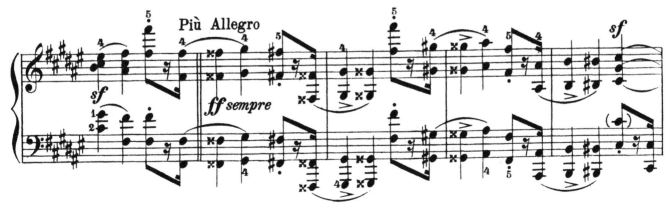

accelerando

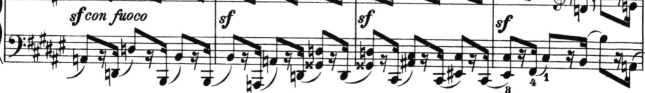

sf con fuoco

sempre accelerando

quasi pizzi.

pp tran-

- cato

- quillo

* to assist the performer, the editors have realized this passage:

dedicated to Madame Henriette Voigt née Kunze

SONATA No. 2

Edited by Clara Schumann

As fast as possible ♩ = 144

Robert Schumann, Op. 22
(1835/38)

50

*) Execution

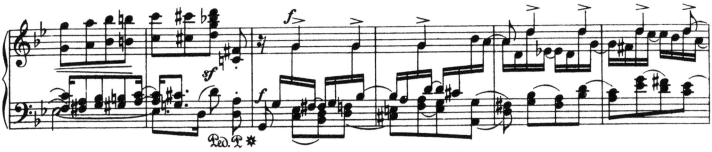

Ancora più vivo

Andantino ♪ = 104

sostenuto

Scherzo
Molto presto e marcato ♩ = 138

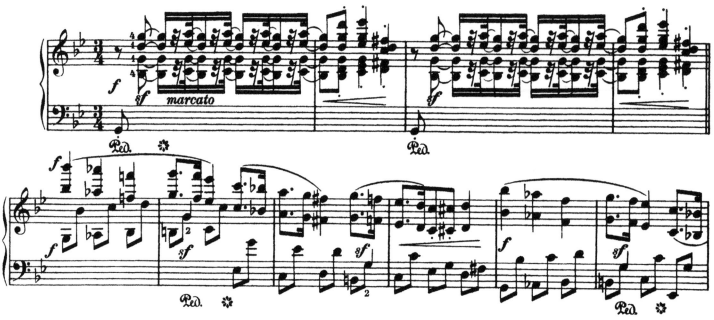

57

Rondo
Presto ♩ = 160

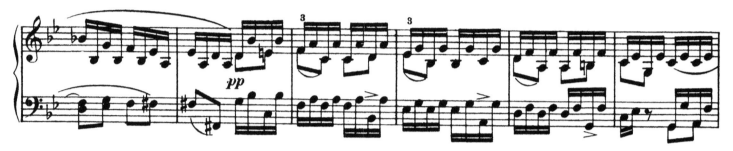

Prestissimo

Quasi Cadenza

dedicated to Monsieur Ignace Moscheles

GRAND SONATA

(Concerto without Orchestra)
composed 1835 (1836) as Sonata No. 2
in four movements

Robert Schumann, Op.14
(1835)

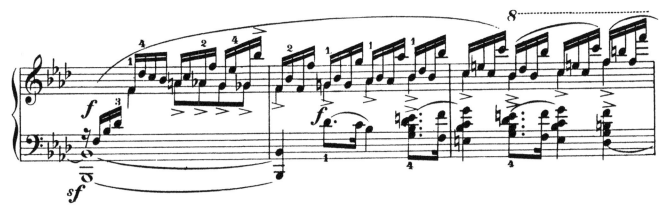

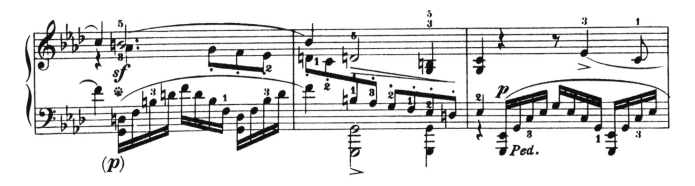

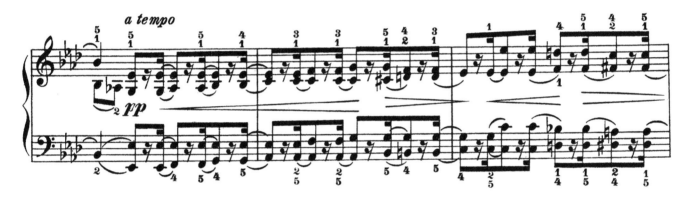

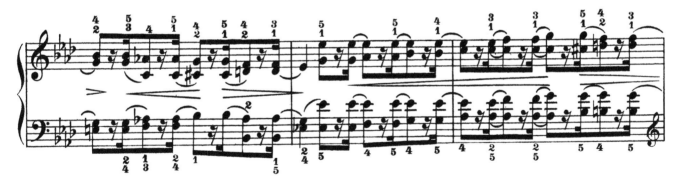

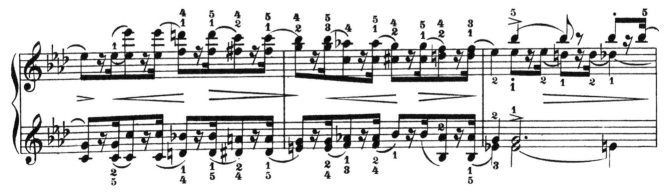

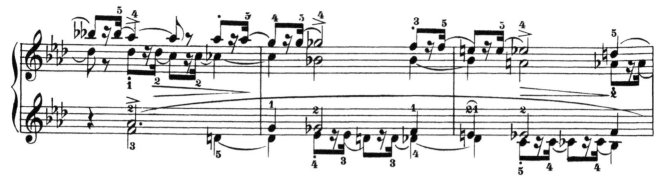

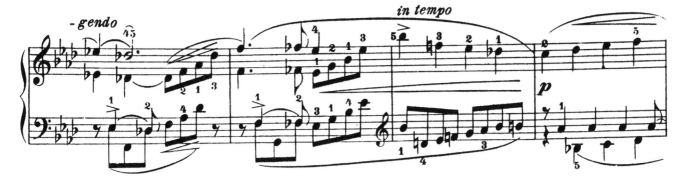

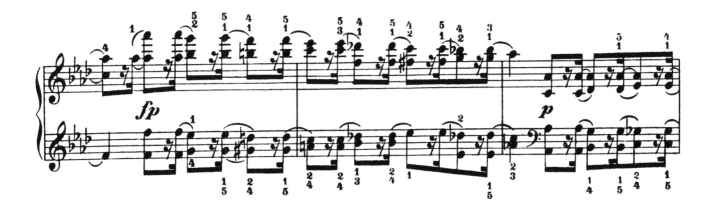

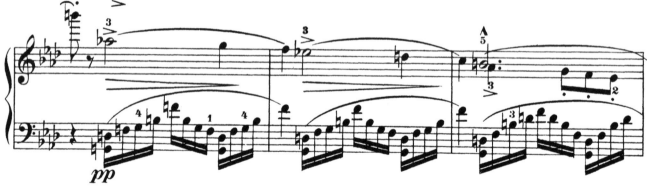

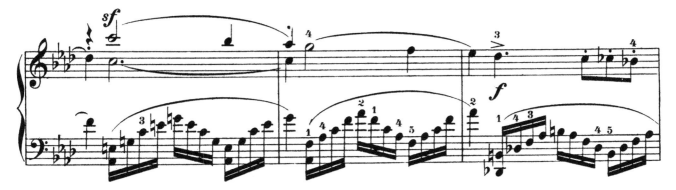

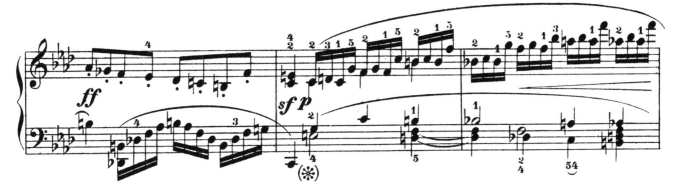

Pedale

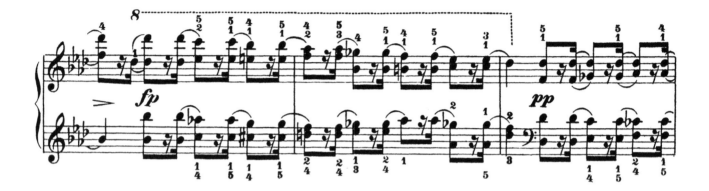

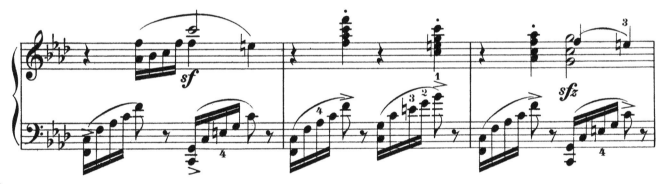

Scherzo
Molto comodo ♩=116

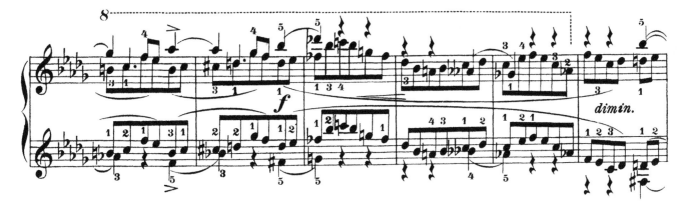

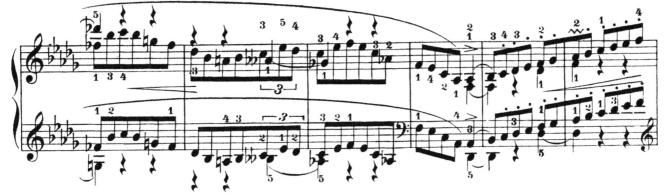

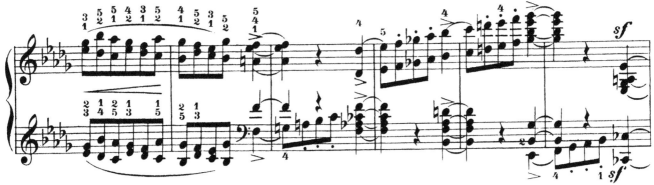

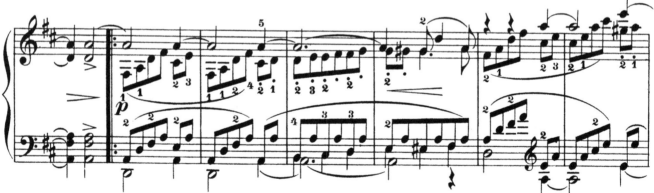

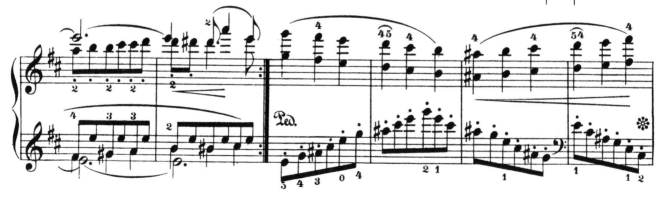

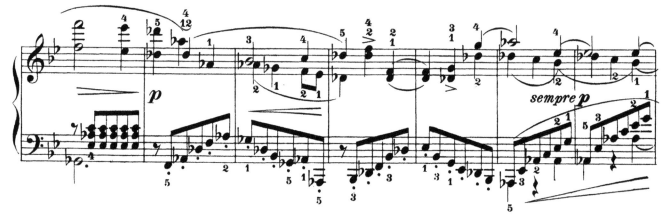

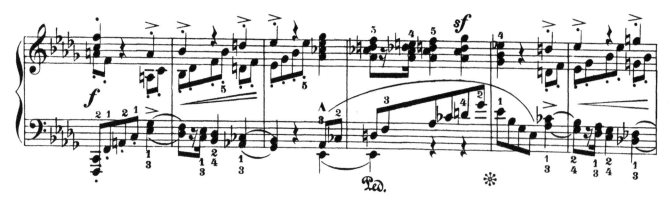

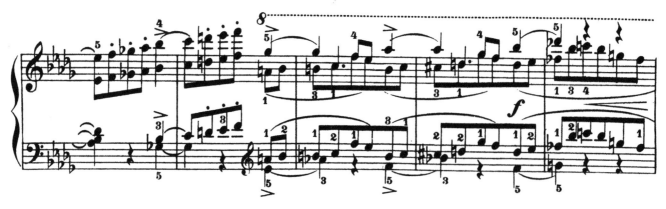

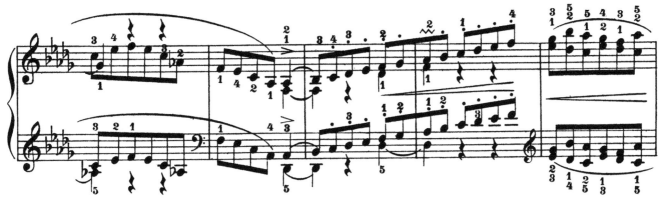

Quasi Variazioni
Andantino de Clara Wieck ♩ = 84

VAR.1

VAR. 2
In tempo

VAR. 3
Passionato (c. ♩=69)

Prestissimo possibile ♩= 96
passionato

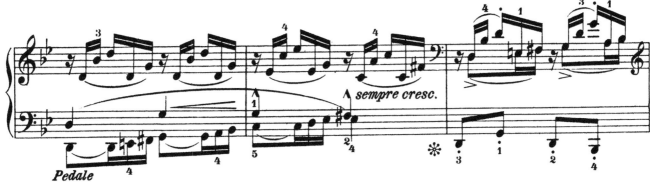

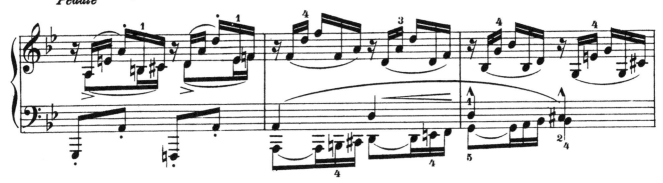

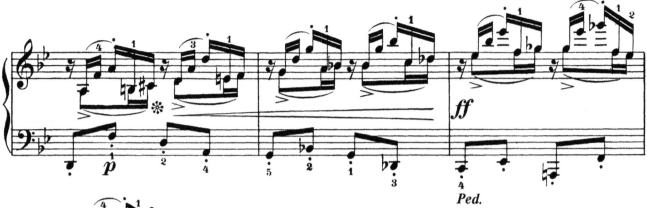

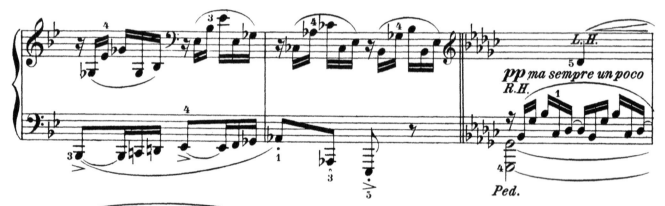

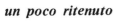

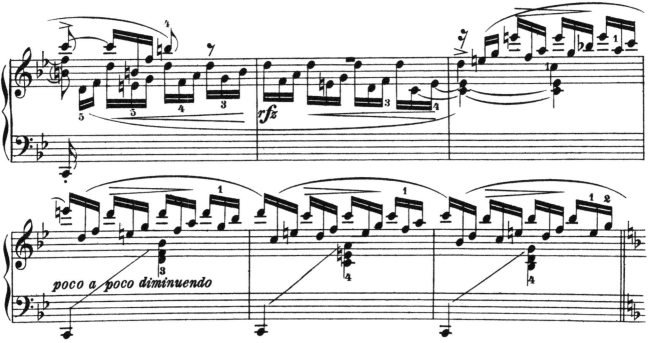

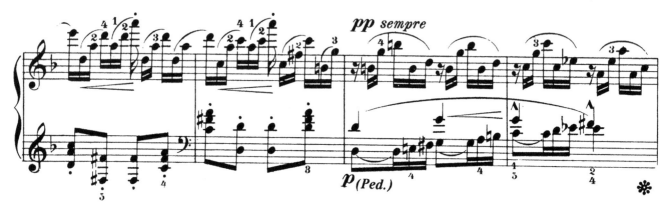

Supplements

SCHERZO

("Scherzo I" for the Concerto without Orchestra, Op. 17)

Robert Schumann, Op.17
(1836)

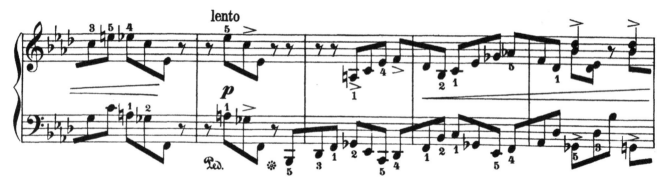

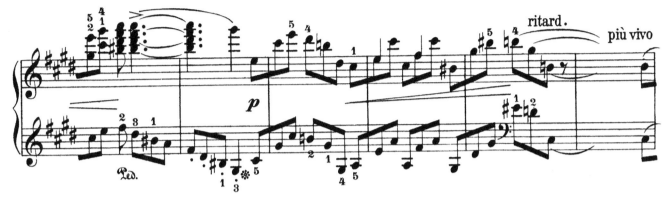

TRIO

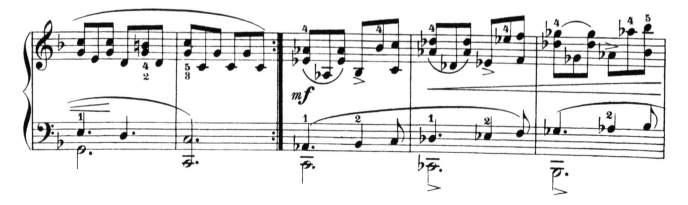

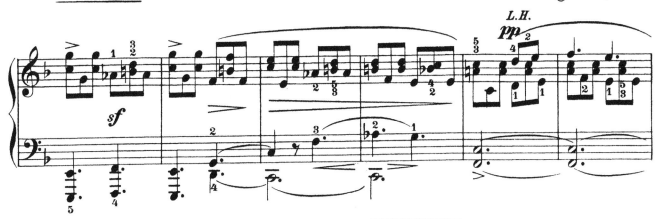

PRESTO

("Finale" for the Sonata, Op.22)

Robert Schumann, Op.22
(1835)

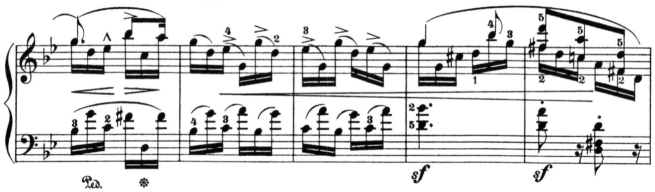

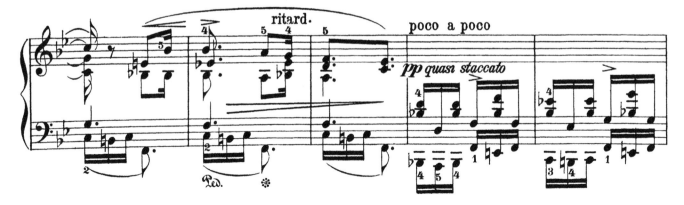

122

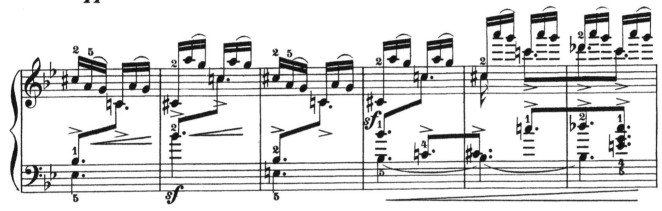

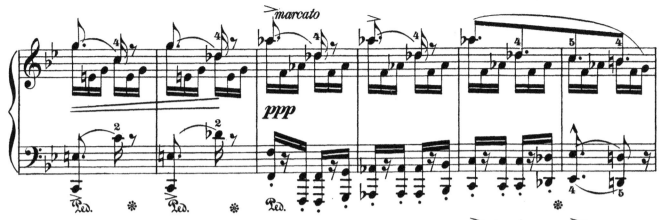

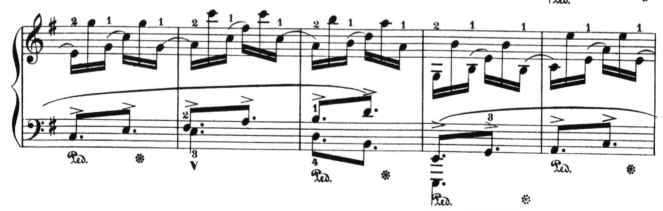